This Book Belongs To :

....

My nose is wet
to help absorb scent chemicals

I spend 70% of my life sleeping

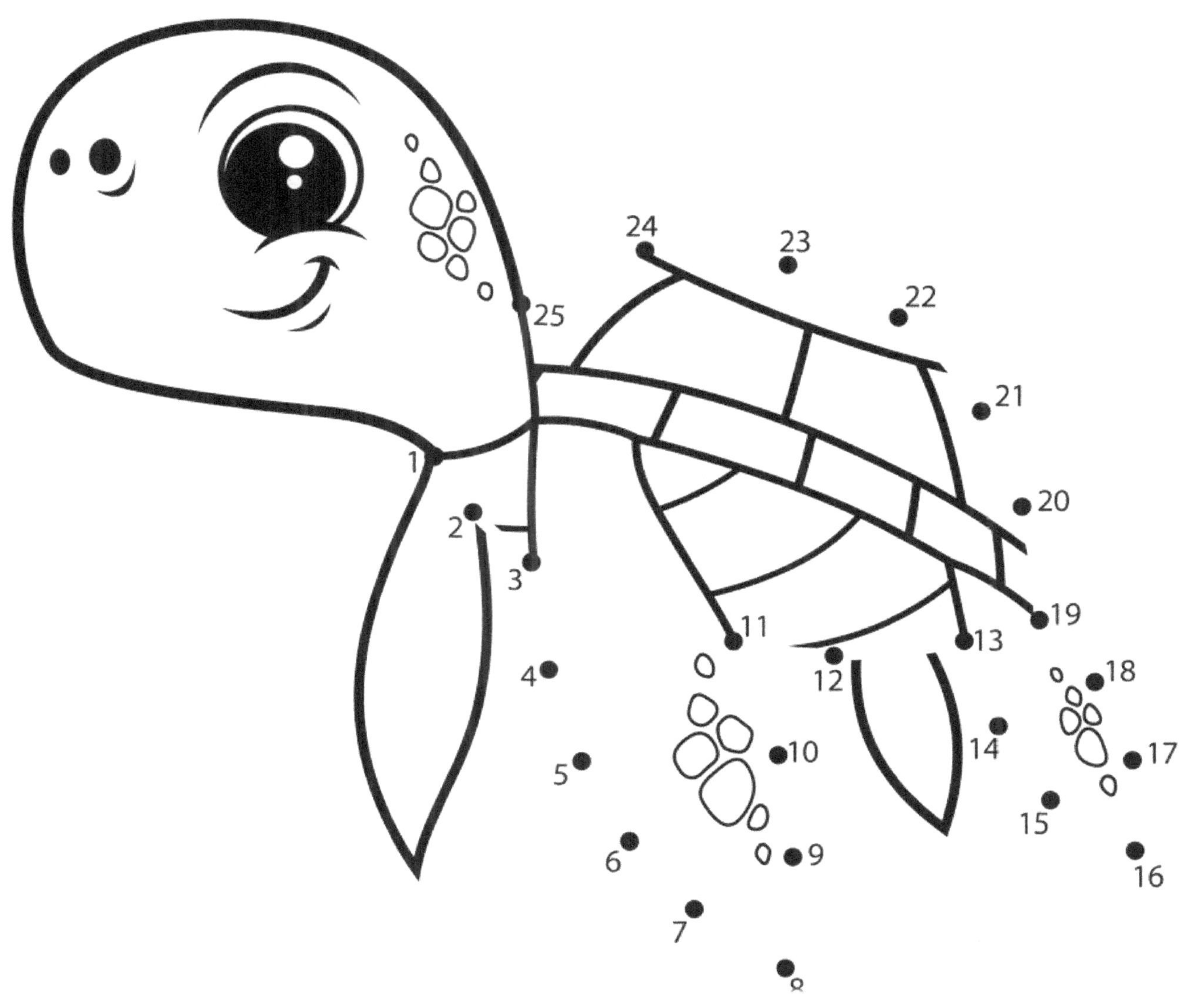

I have lived on Earth for over 100 million years

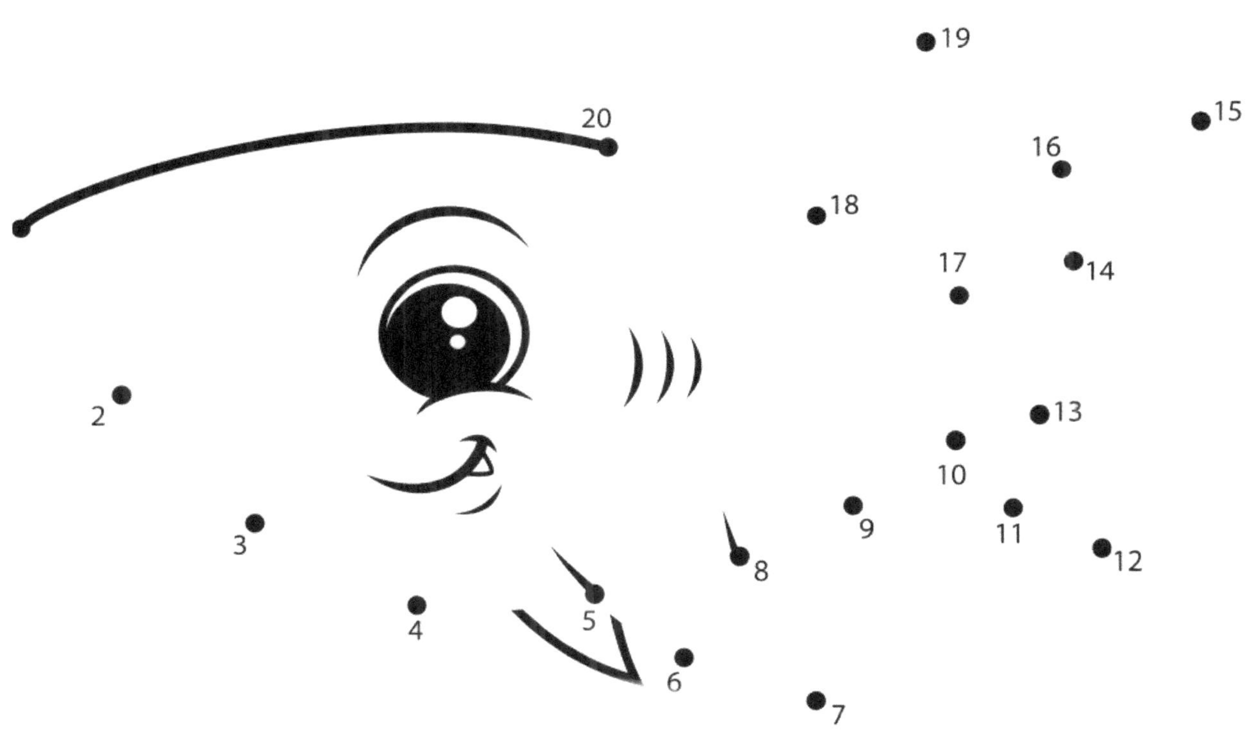

I don't have bones

I taste with my feet

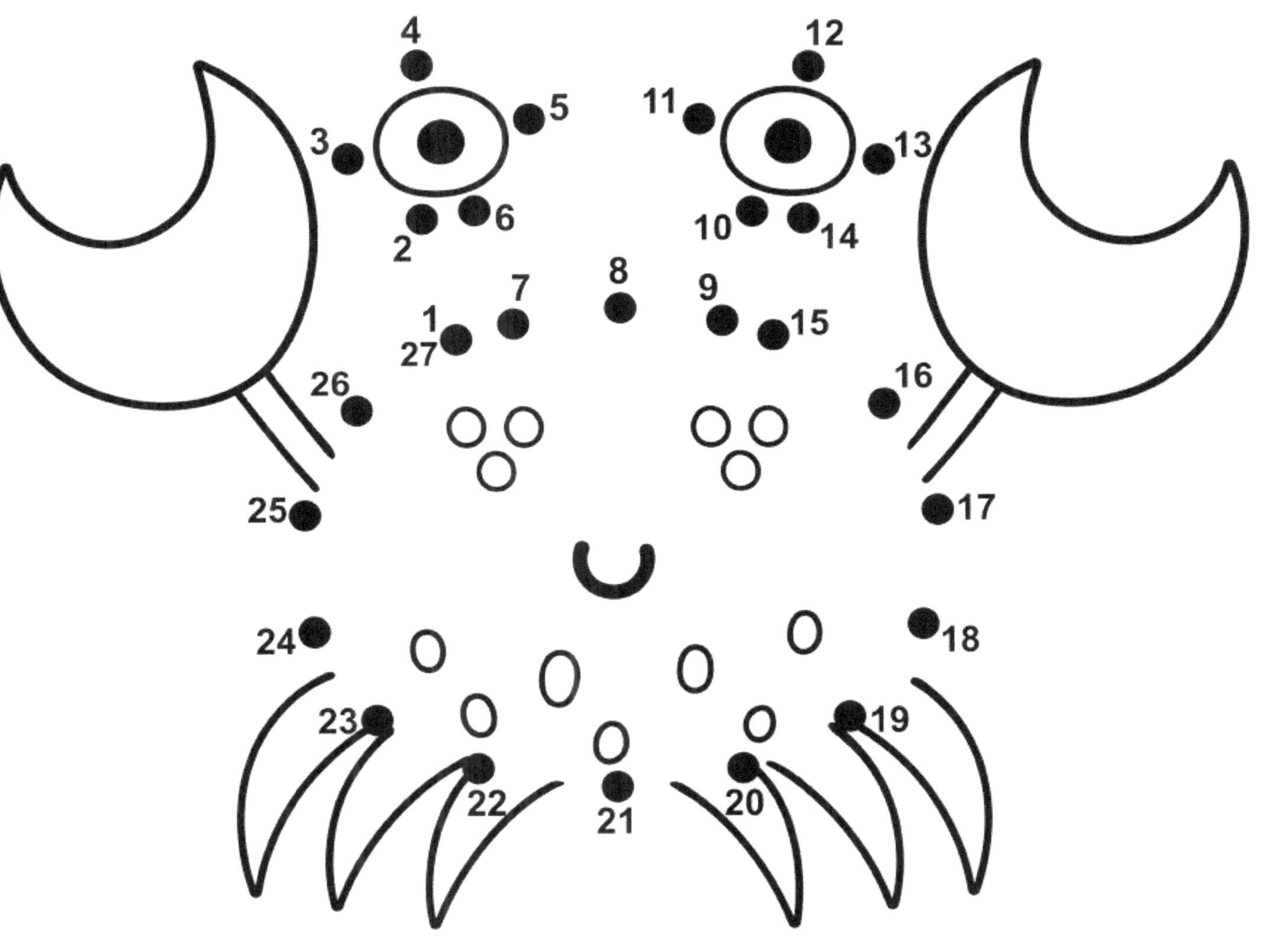

I live in coastal areas of salty, fresh or brackish water

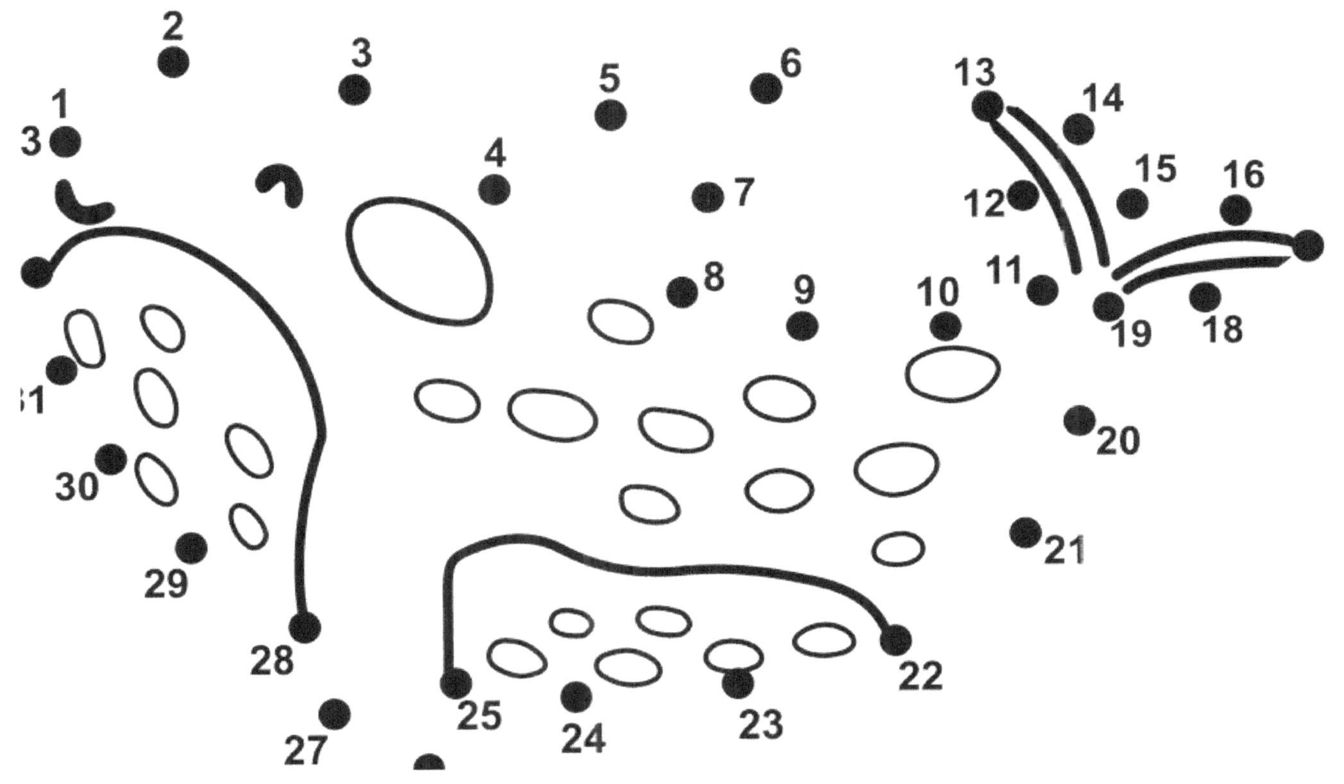

I am the largest animal on earth

I get my name from the bold color
strokes on my body

I have three hearts and
nine brains

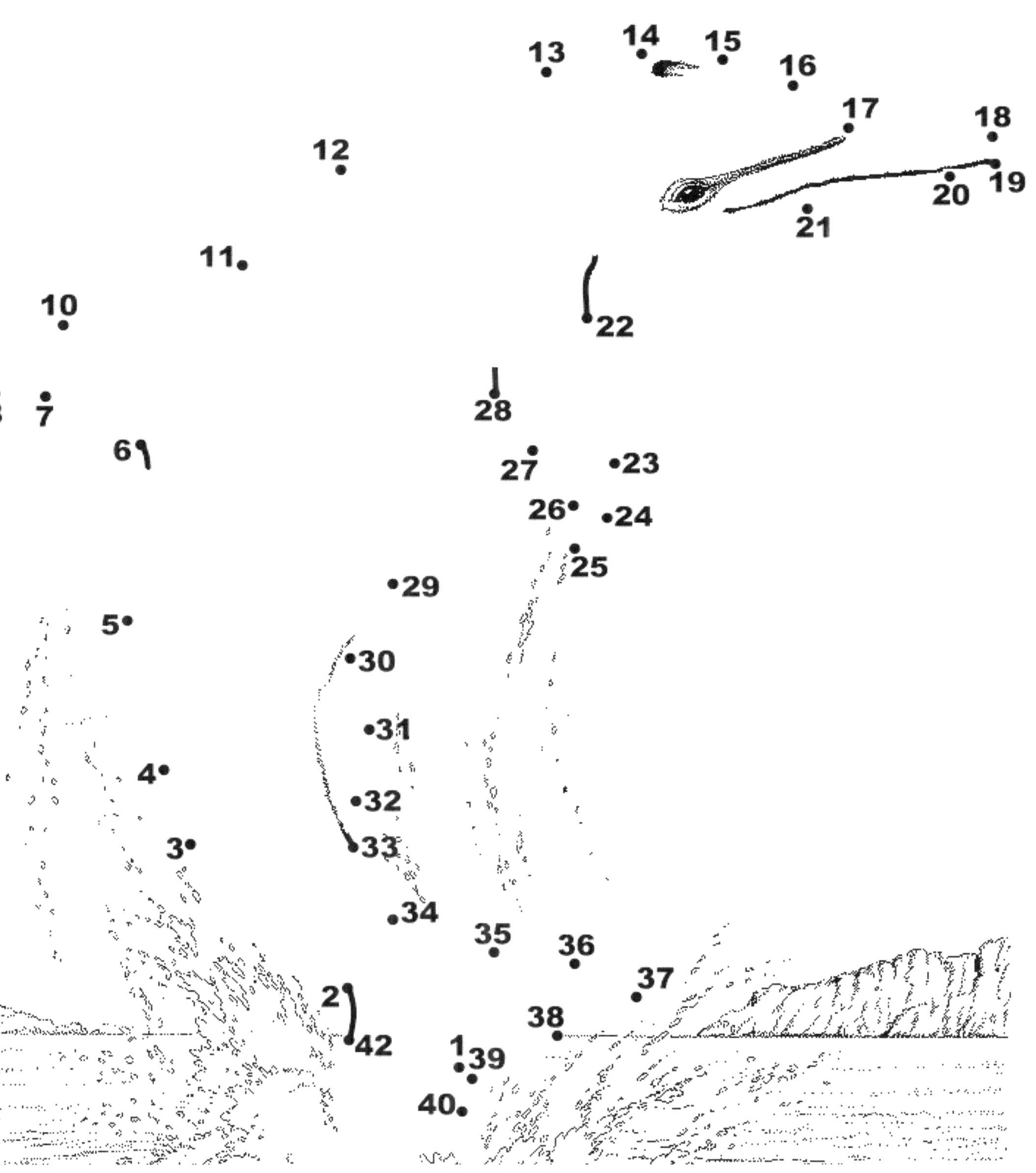

Known for my playful behavior,
I am highly intelligent

My head looks like the head of a
tiny horse

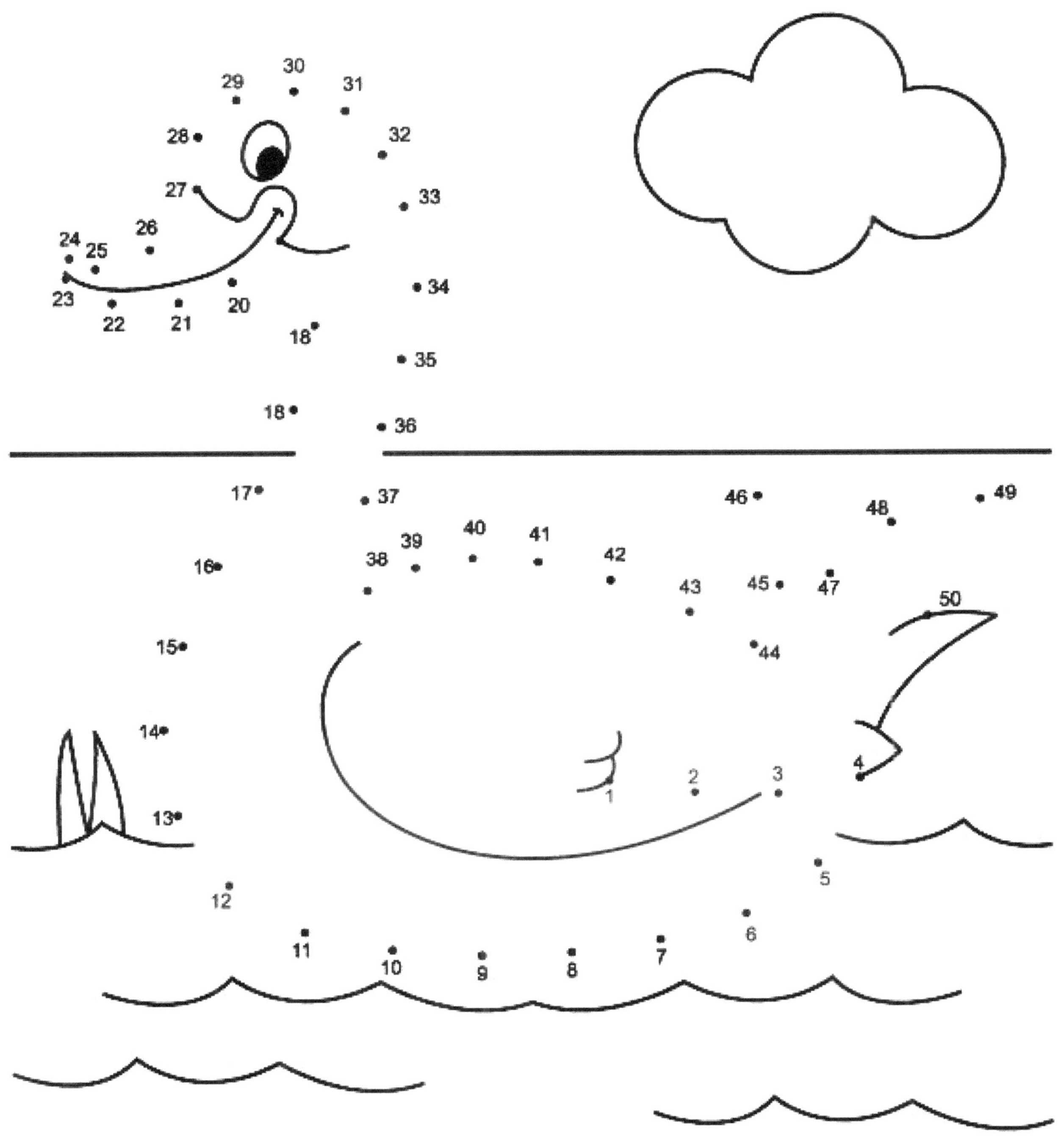

I live about 5 years, and possibly up to 10 year

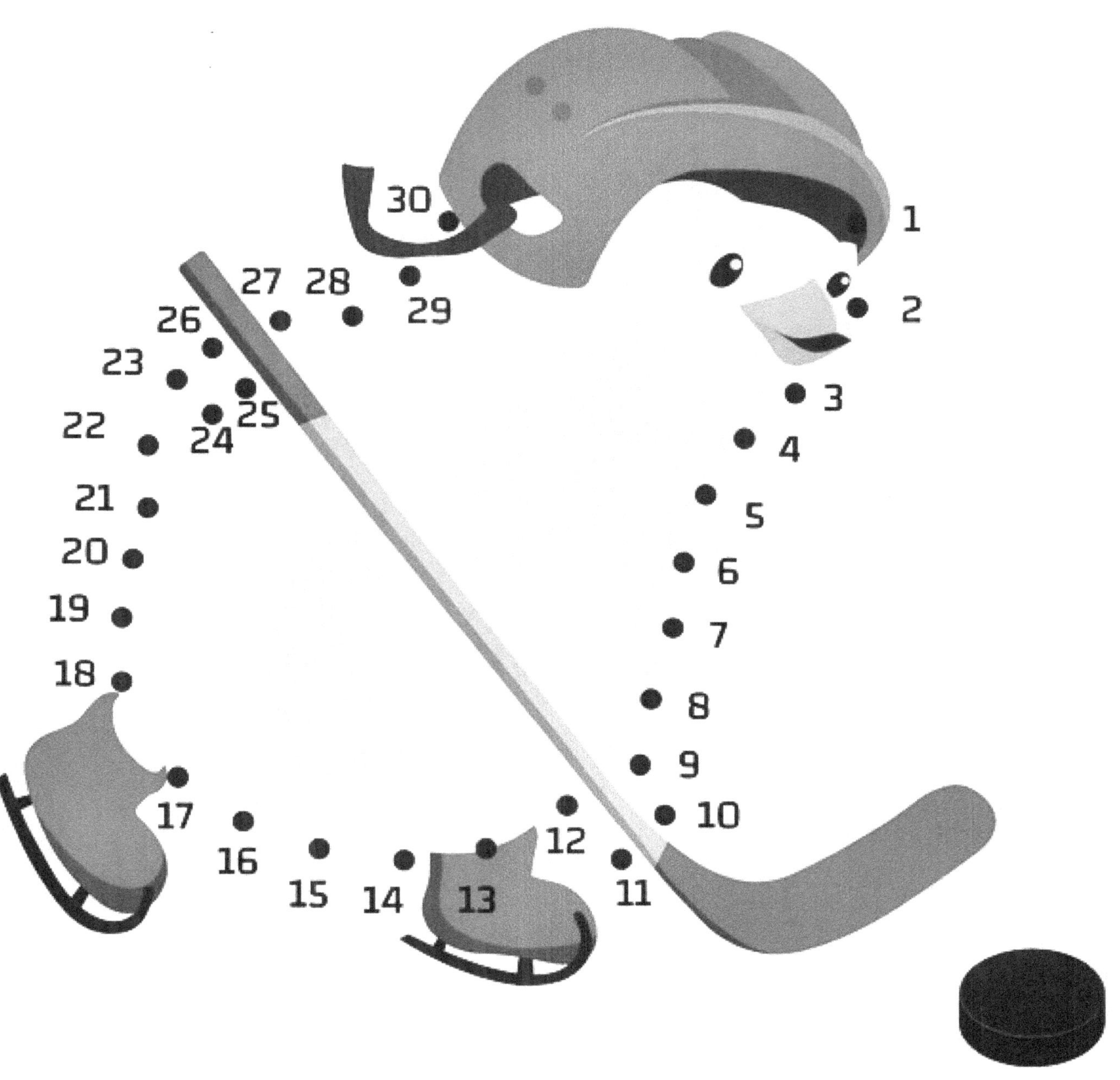

I lost the ability to fly millions of years ago

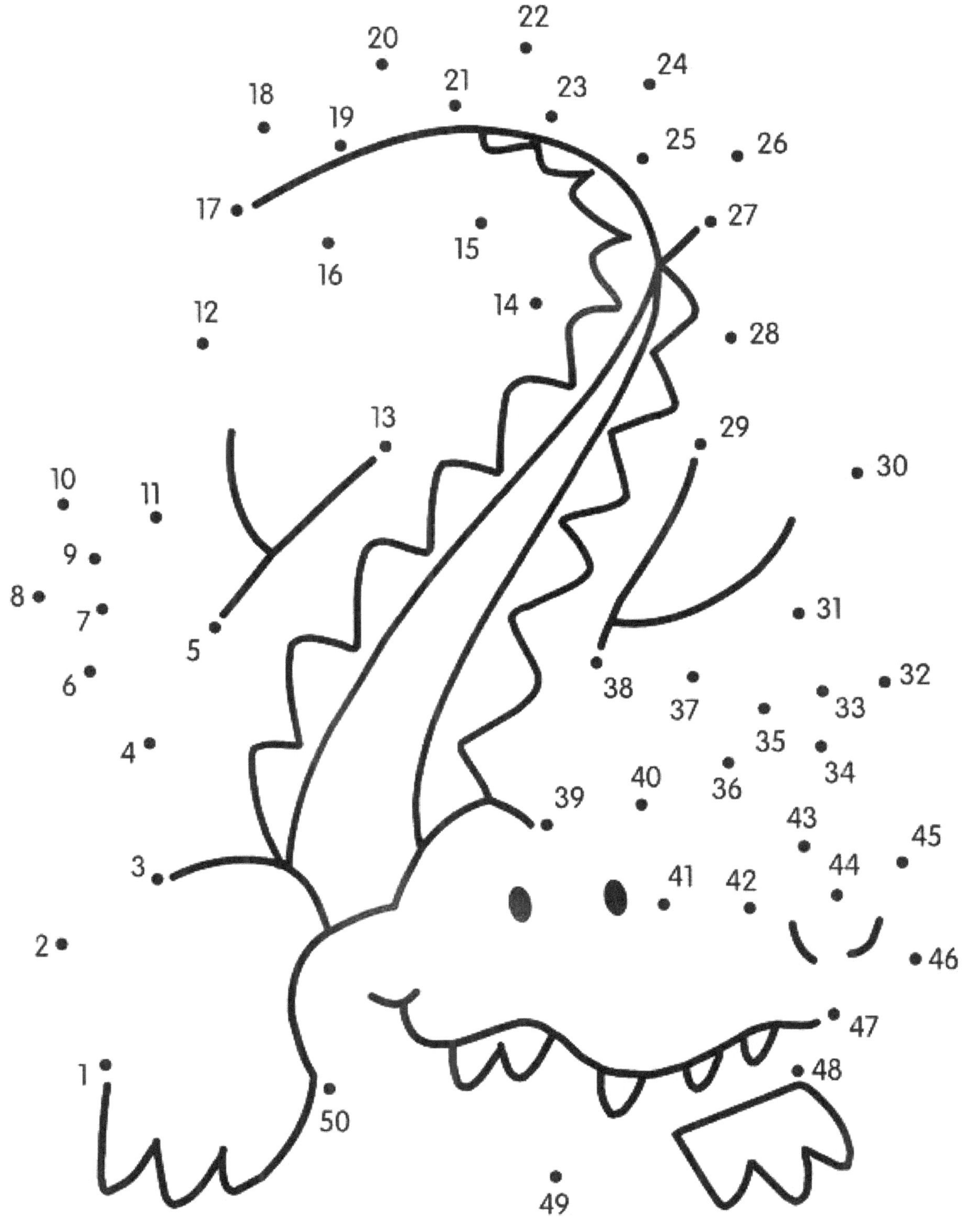

I am closely related todinosaurs
and birds

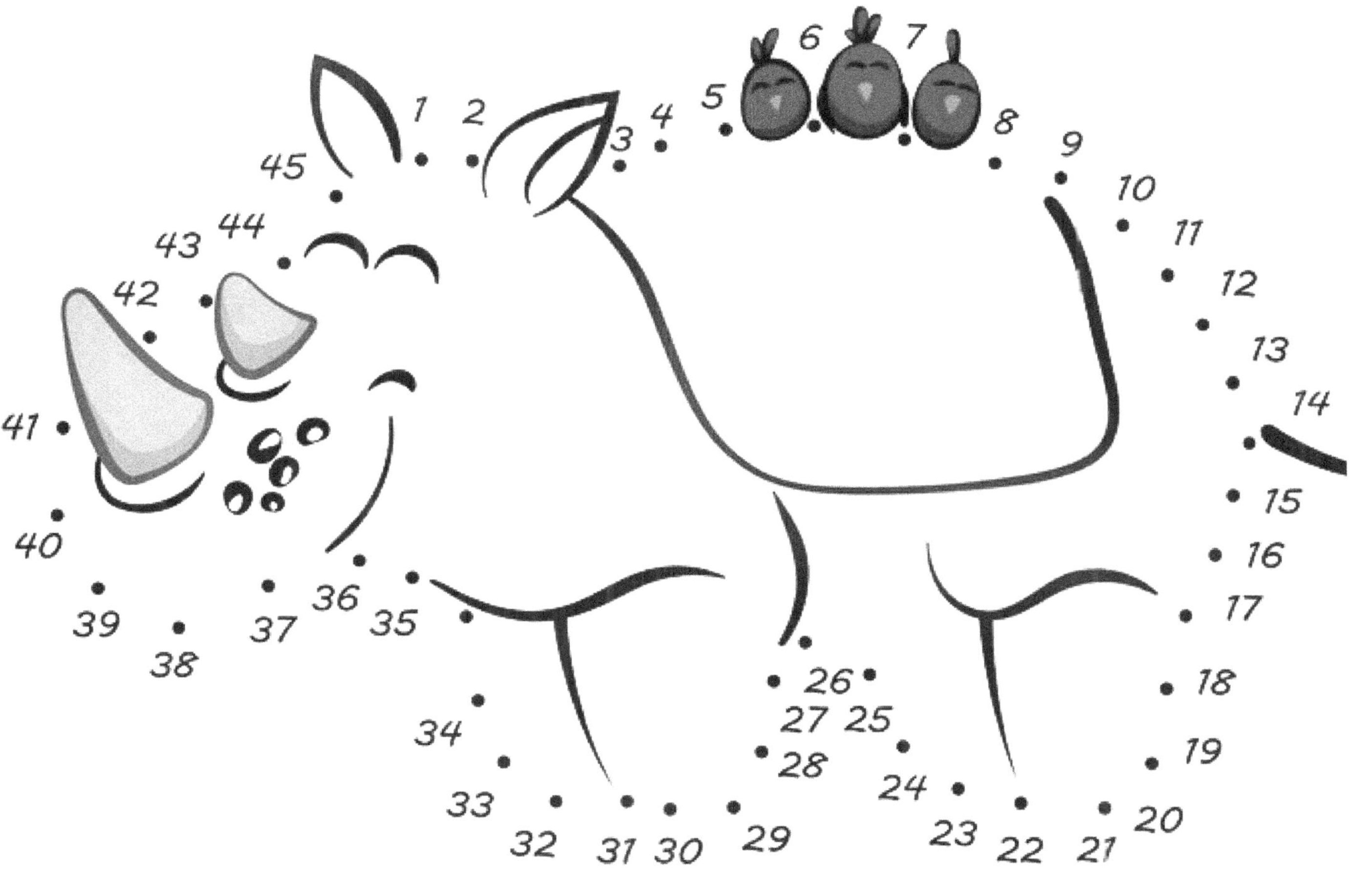

I can grow to weigh over
1000 kg

I have a uniue pattern of
black and white stripes

I am slow but efficient

I weigh around 180 kg

I contain potassium and Vitamin A

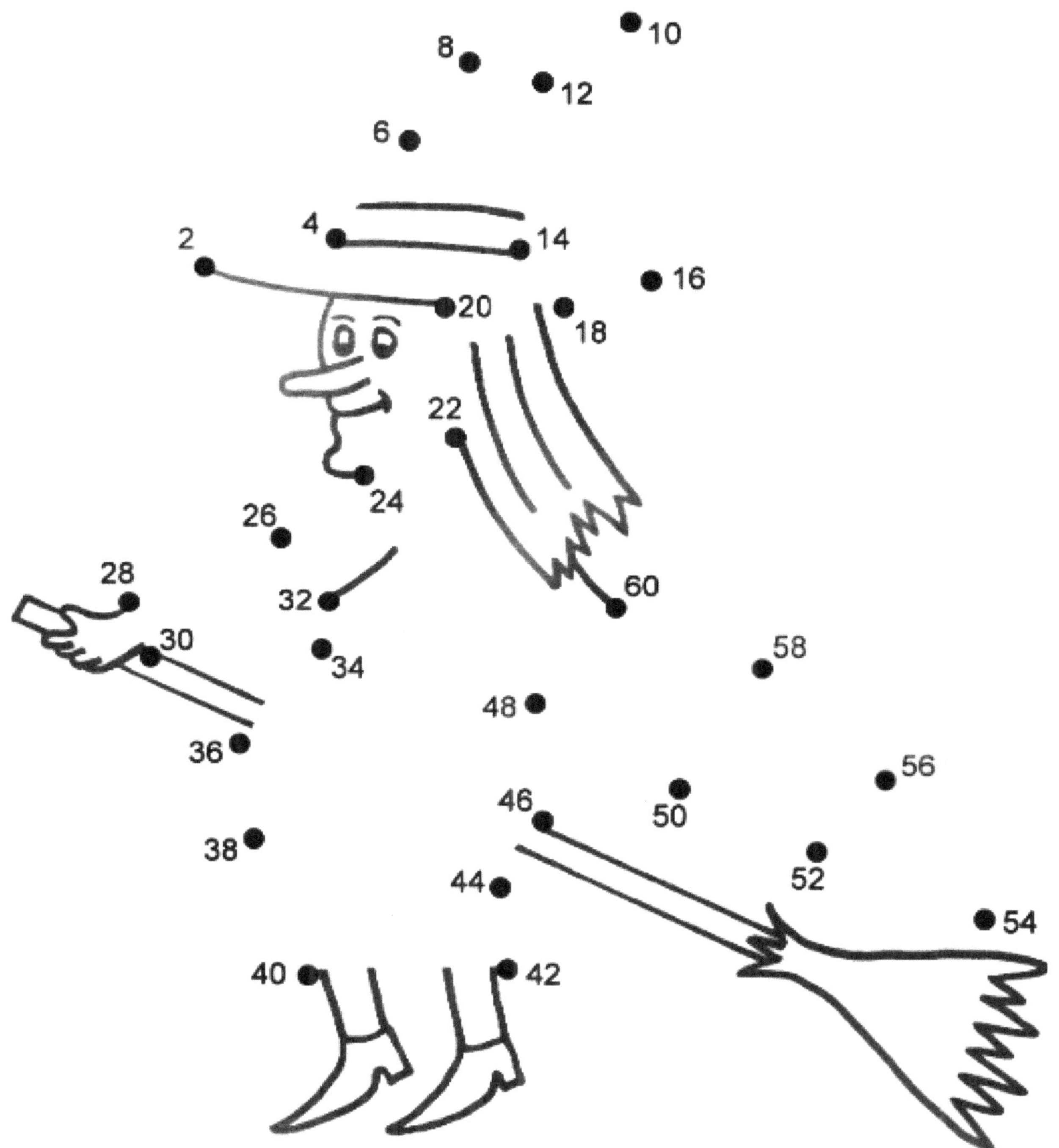

The thing that keeps
me from flying off into the sky
is gravity

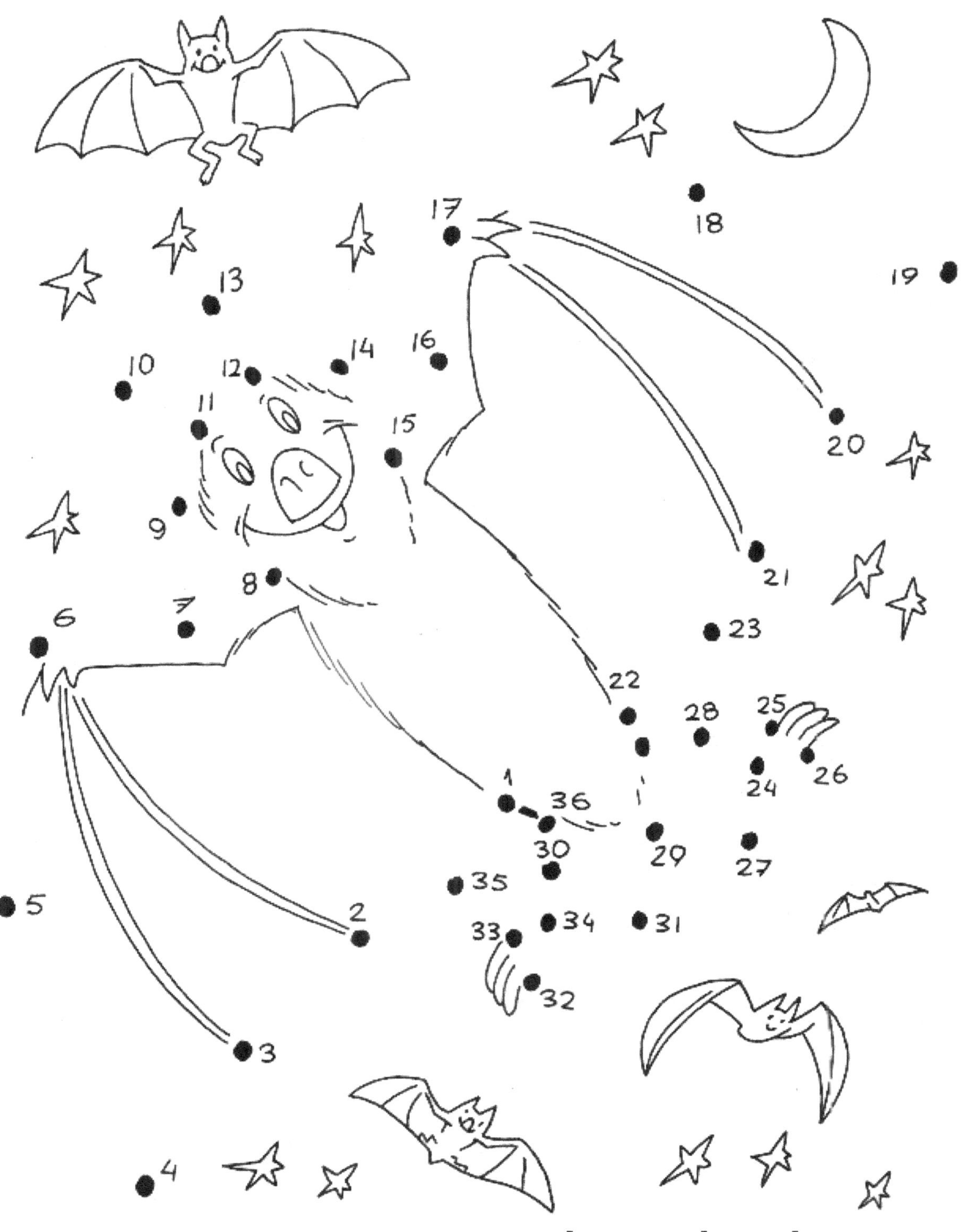

I can see in the dark

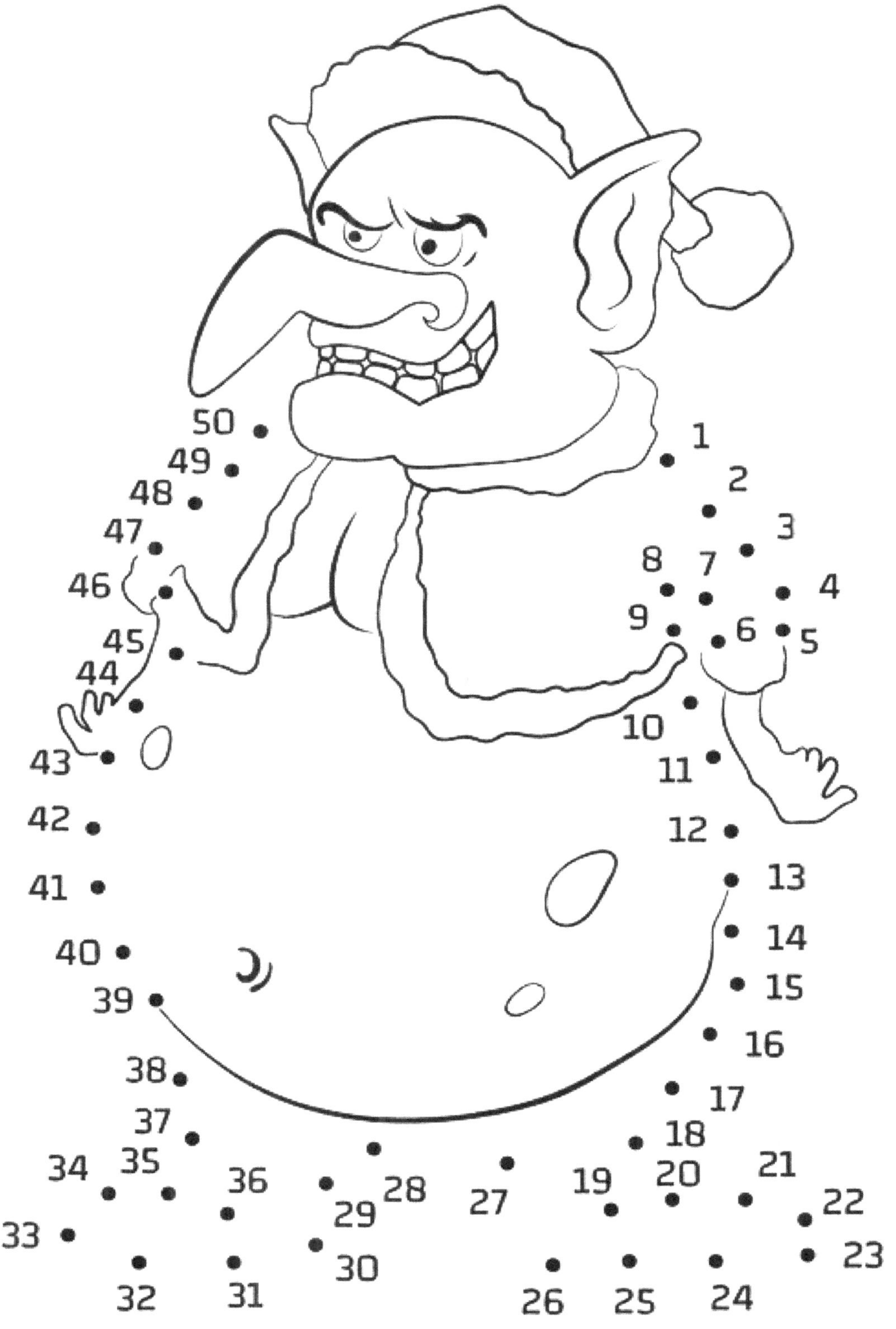

I was supposed to be green

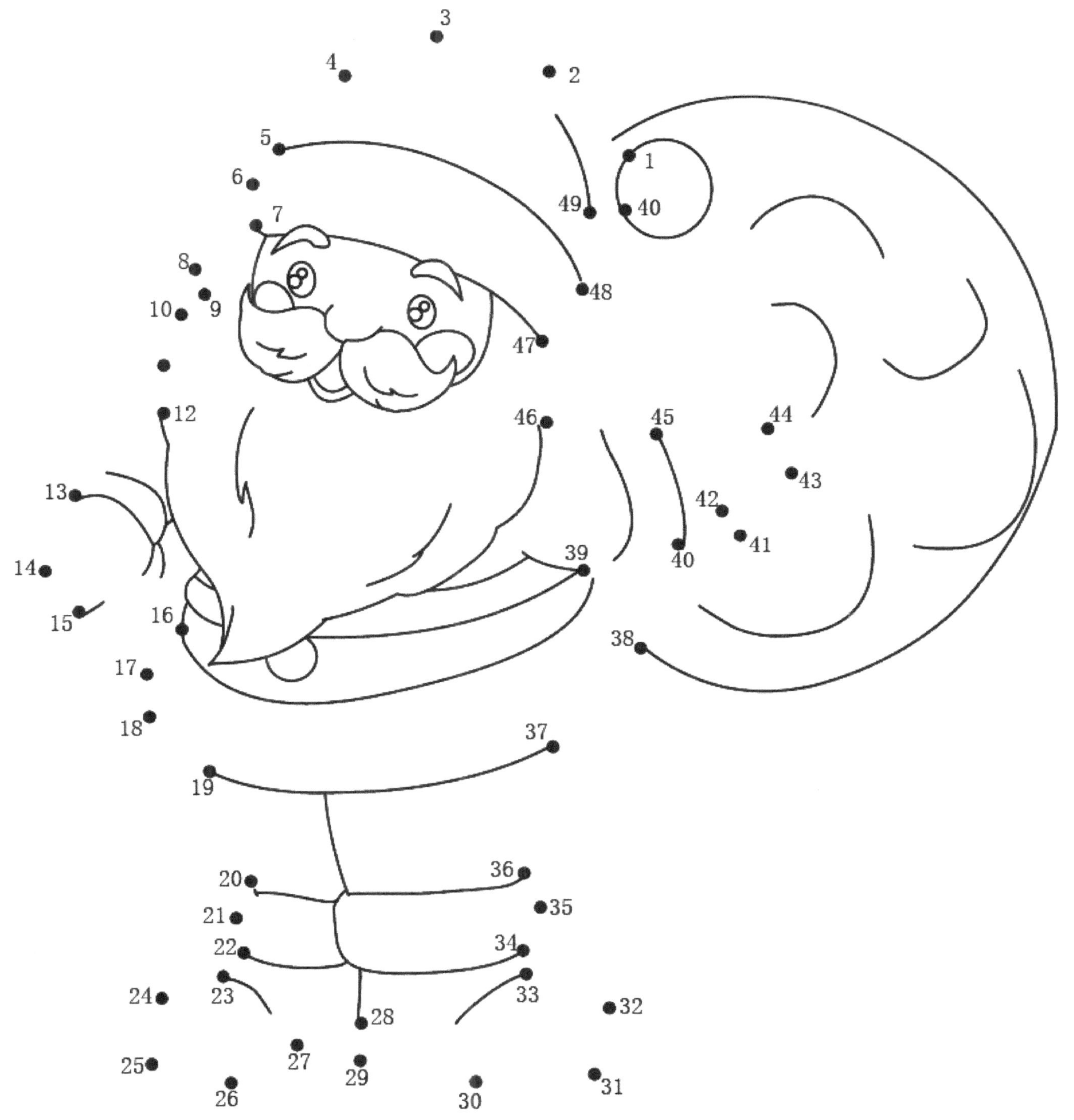

I bring gifts to the homes of
well-behaved children

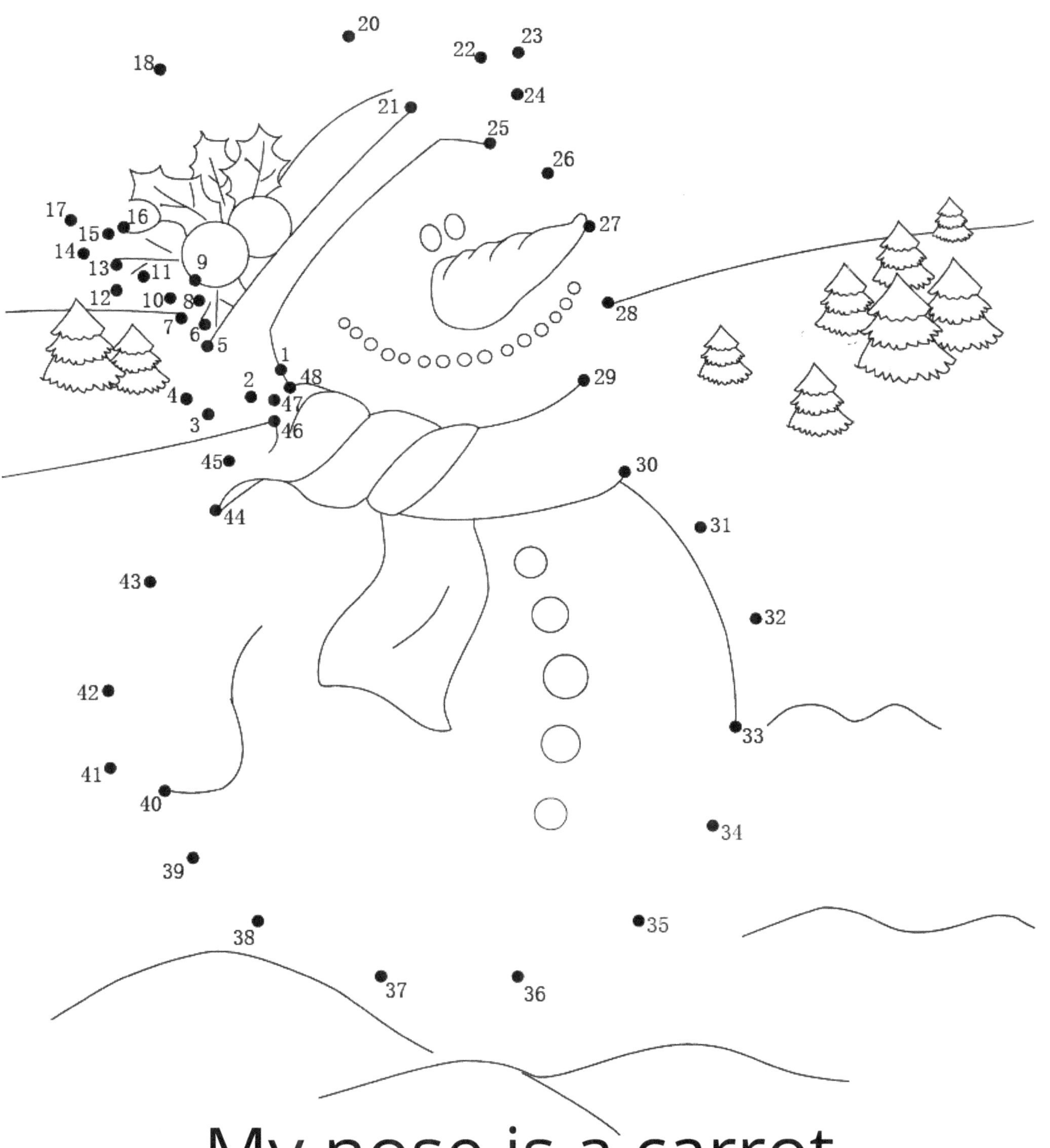

My nose is a carrot

I am celebrated on
December 25

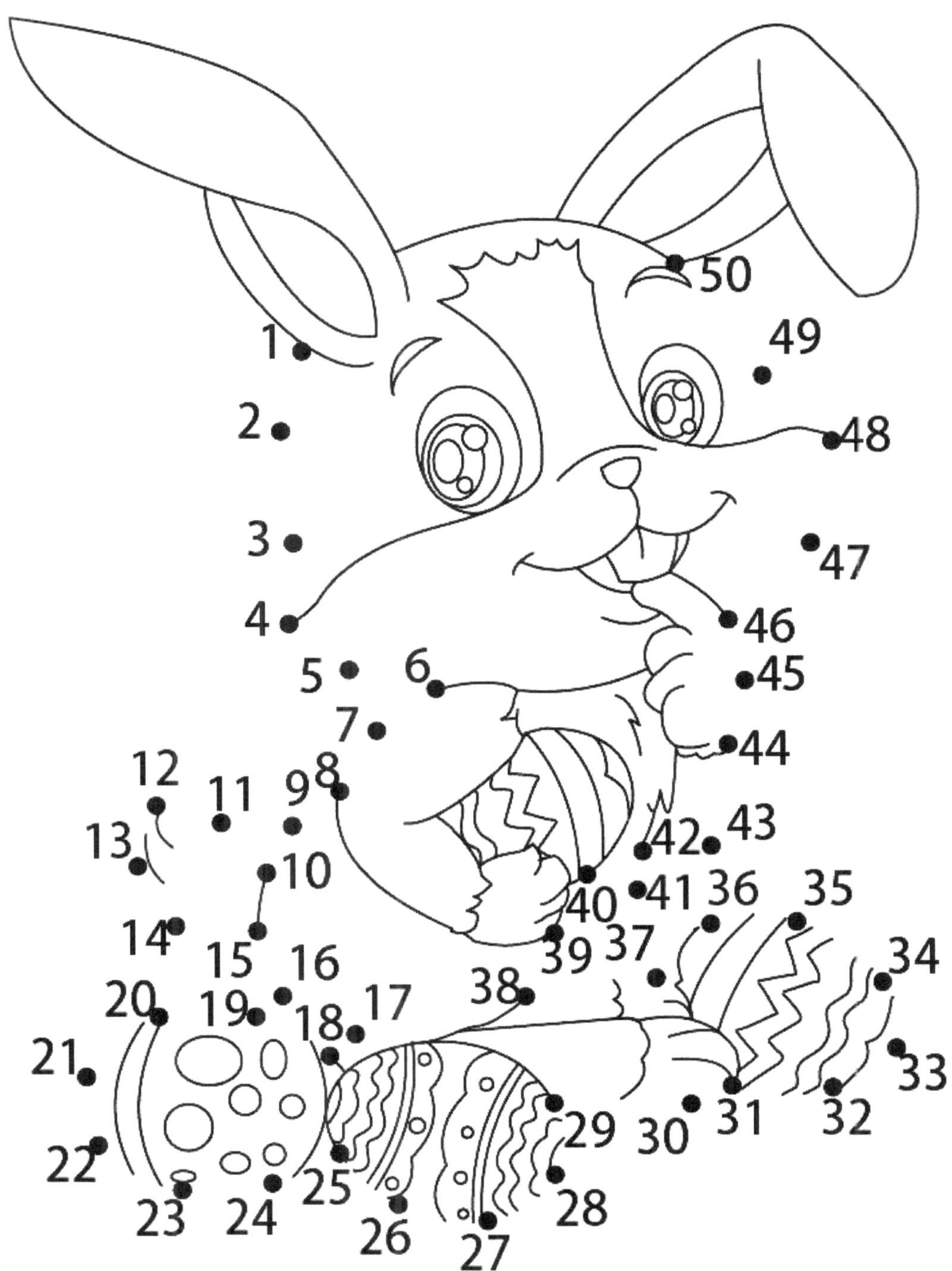

I was first mentioned as an
egg-bringer in 1682

I eat berries, seeds and insects

My front teeth never
stop growing

I can rotate my head 270 degrees

I have sharp Teeth

I weight more than 45 kilos

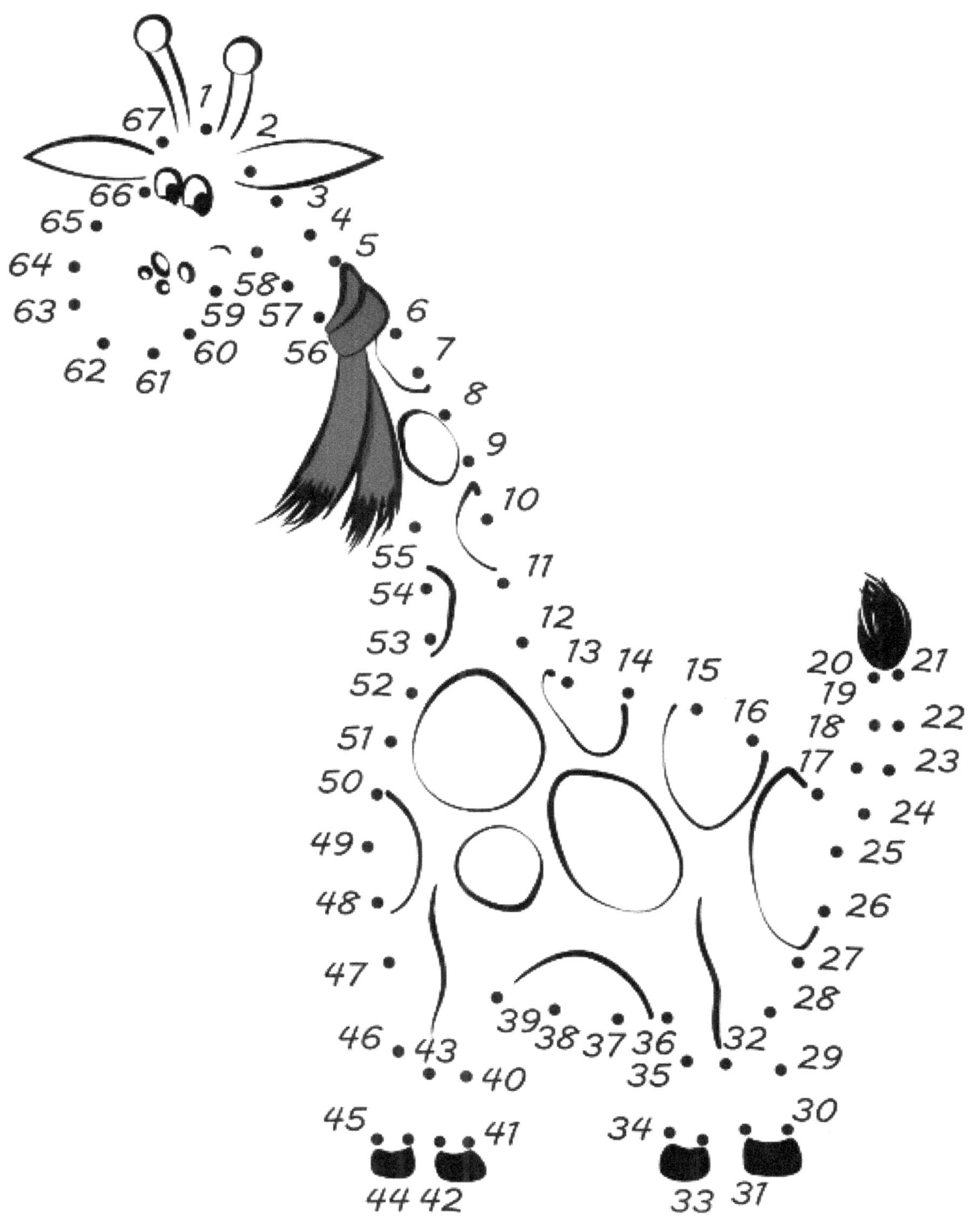

I am the tallest mammal
on Earth

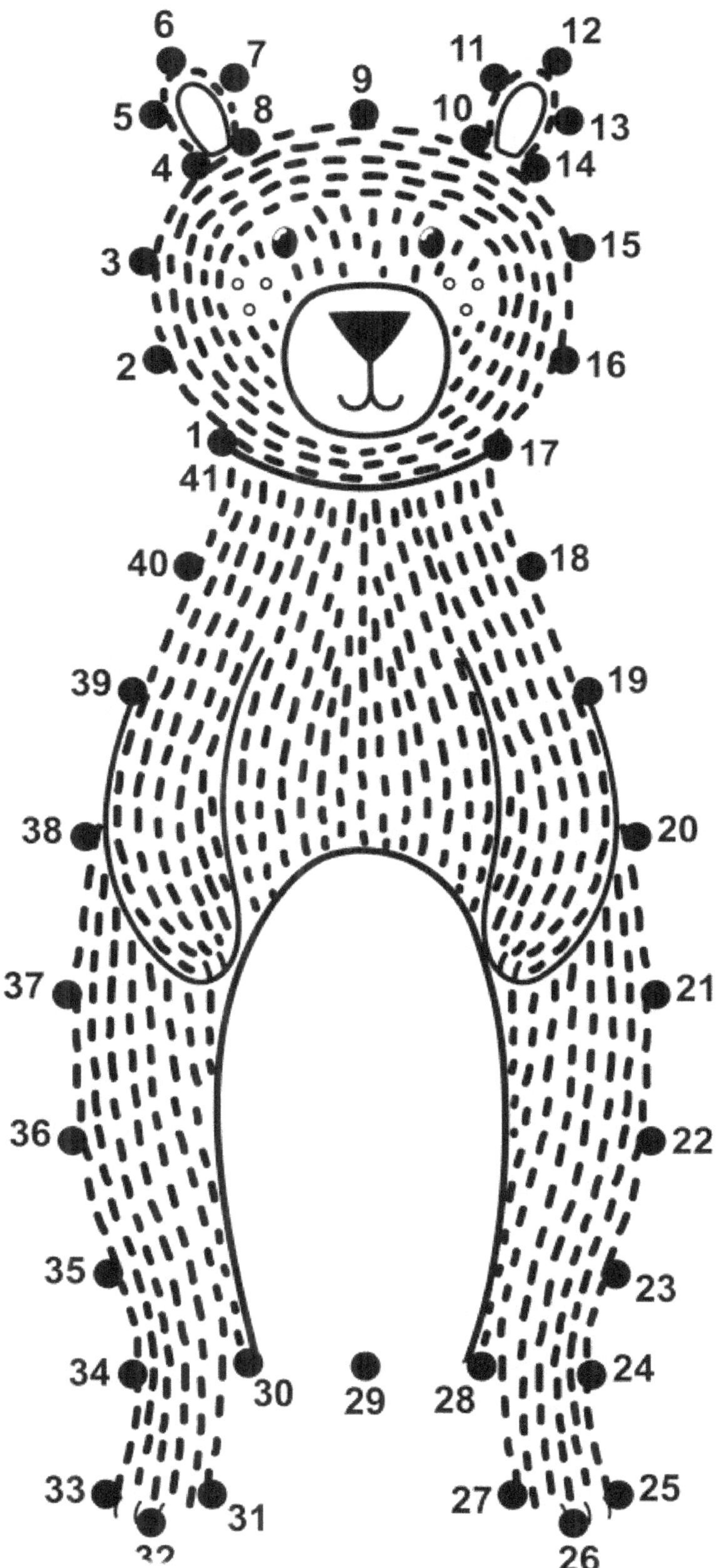

I can run at the speed up to 35mph

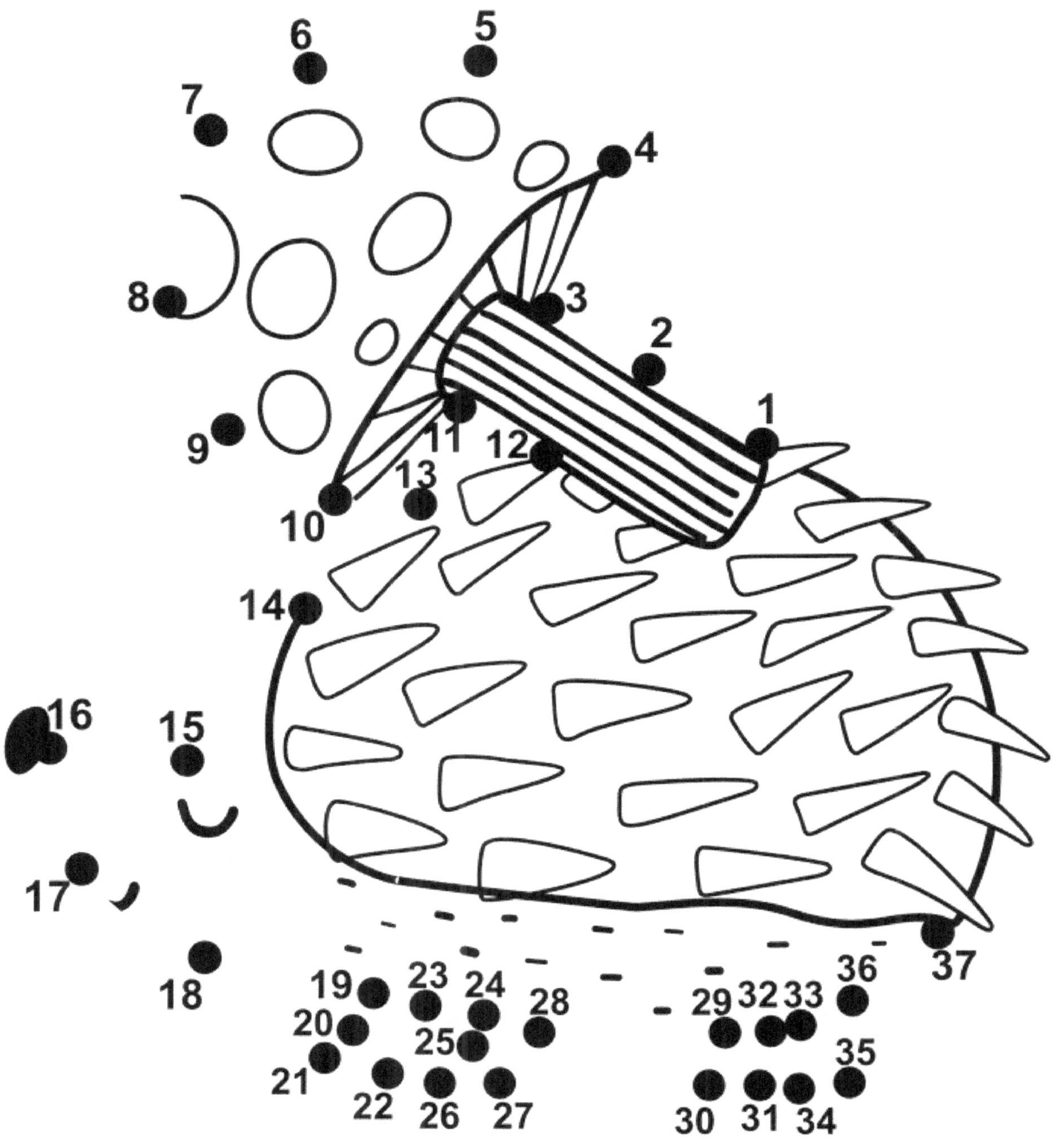

I sleep during the day

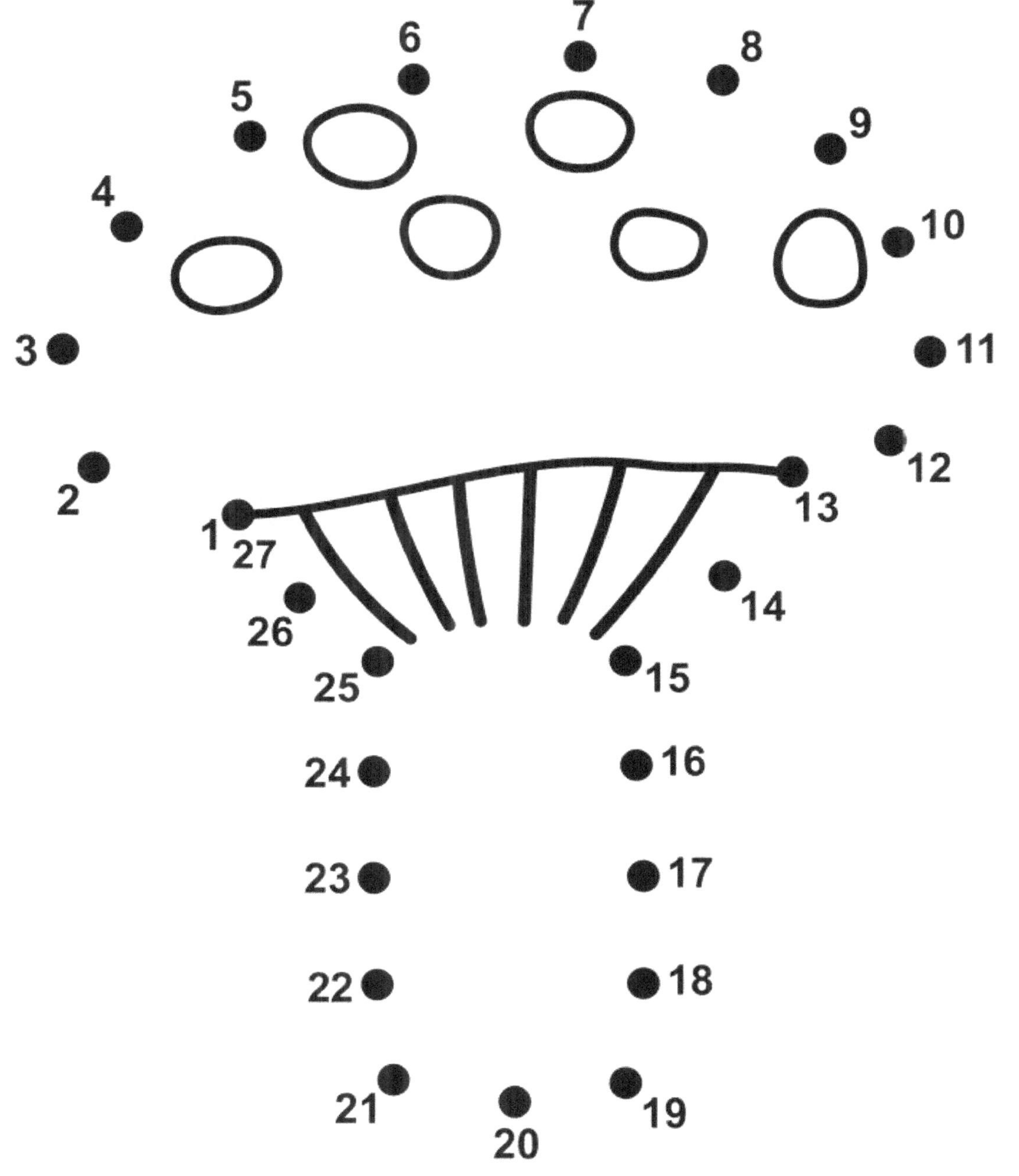

I am made up of around 90% water

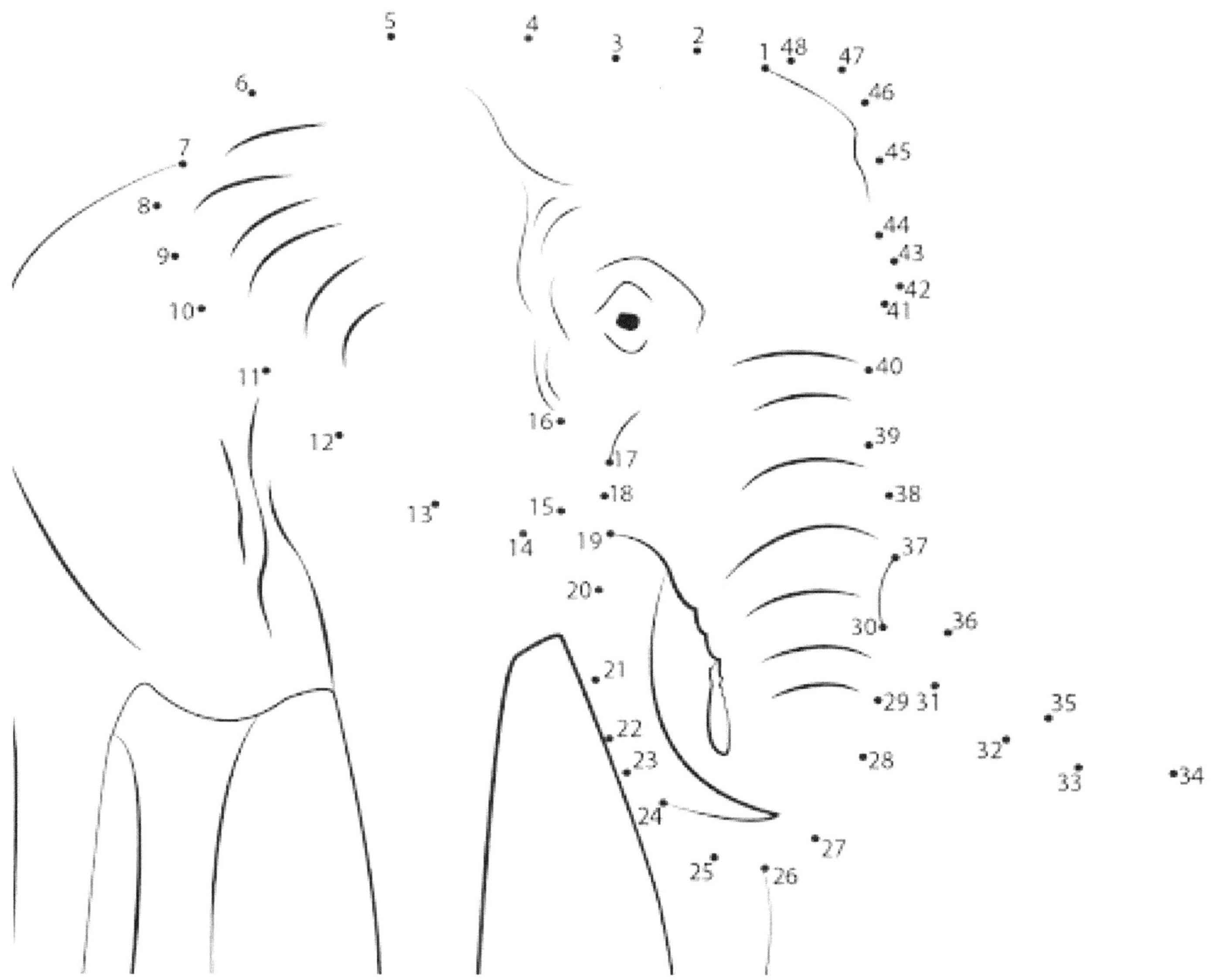

I am the largest living land mammal in the world

I use my tail for balance

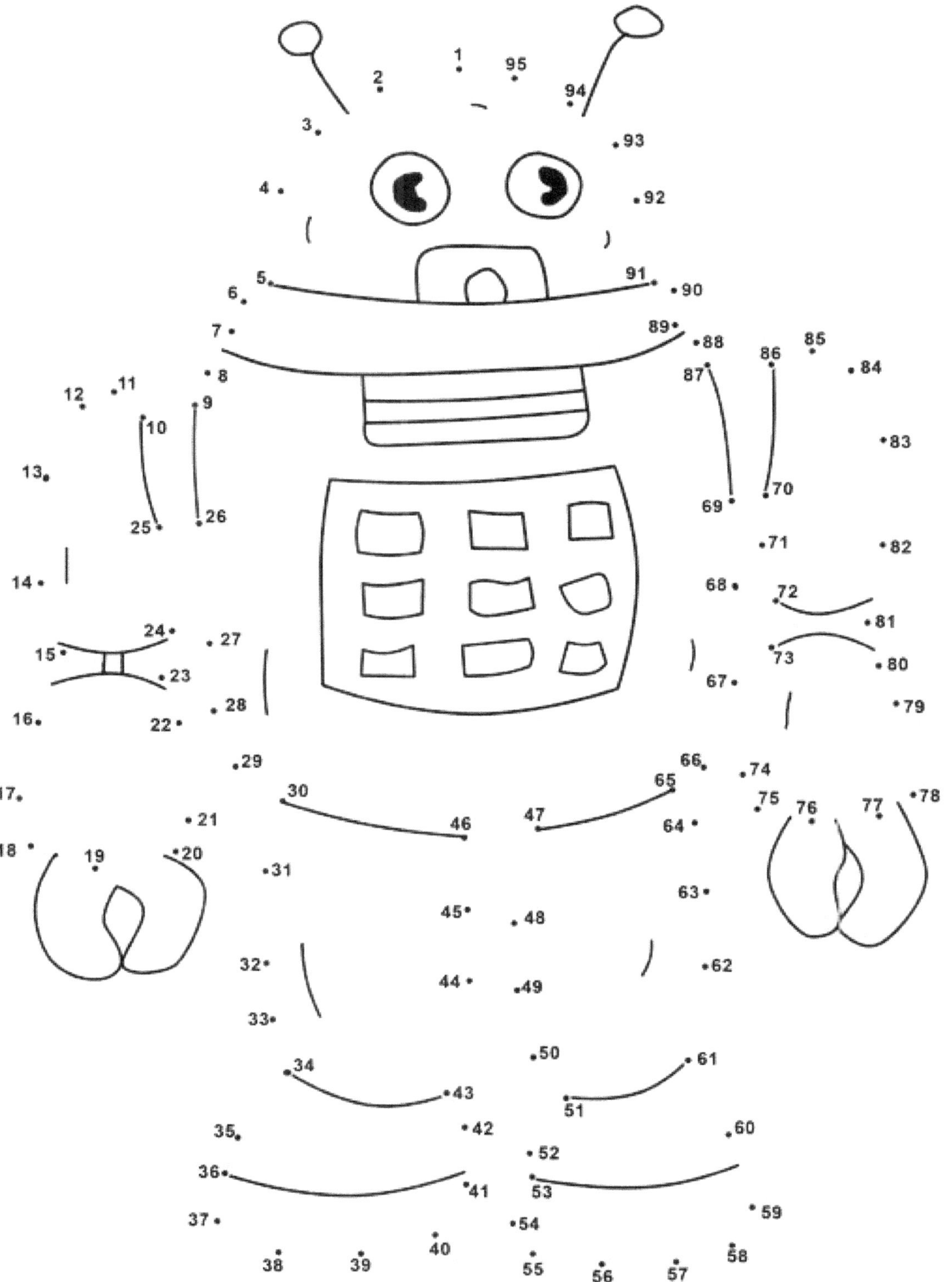

I was invented in 1954

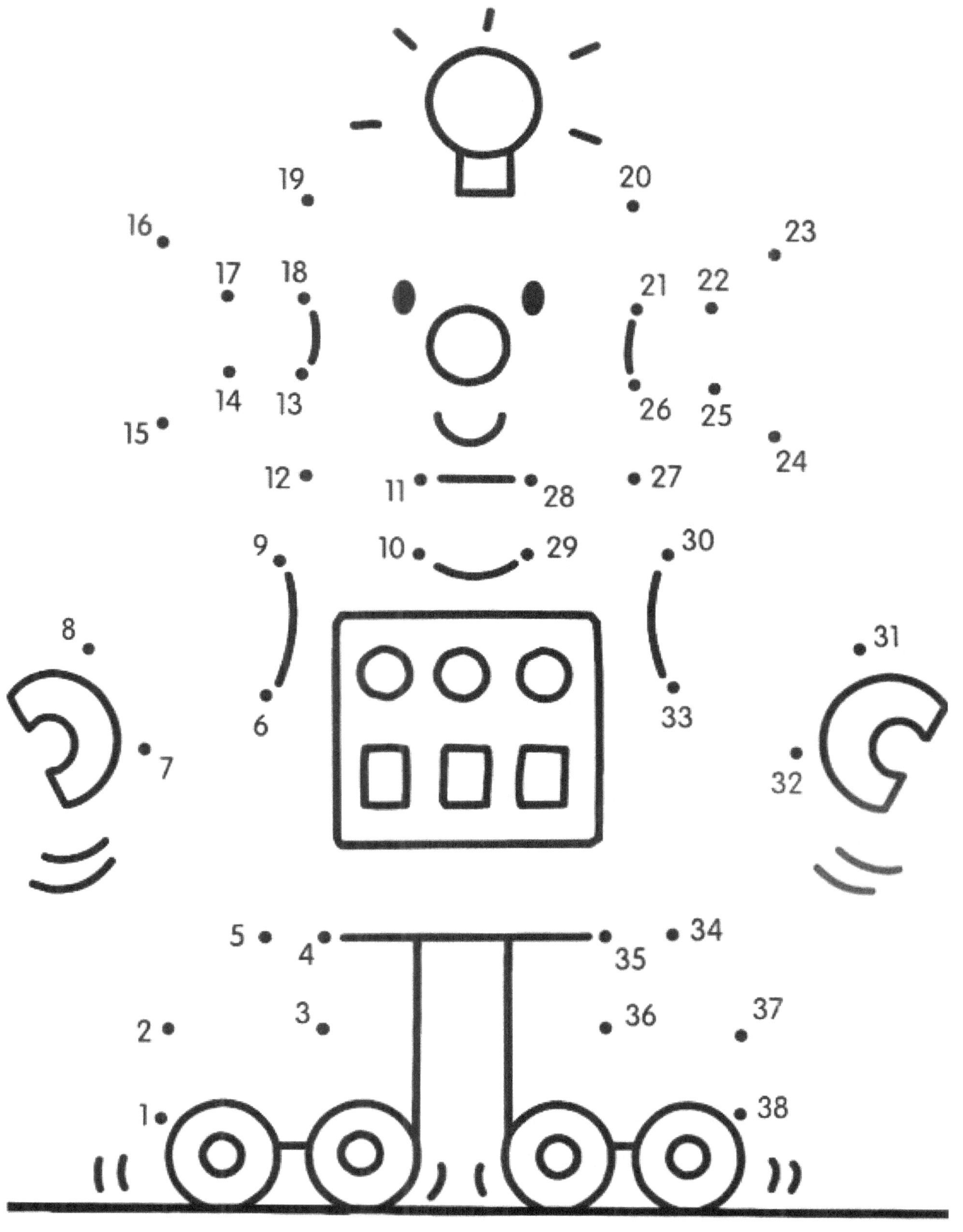

I was invented by George Devol

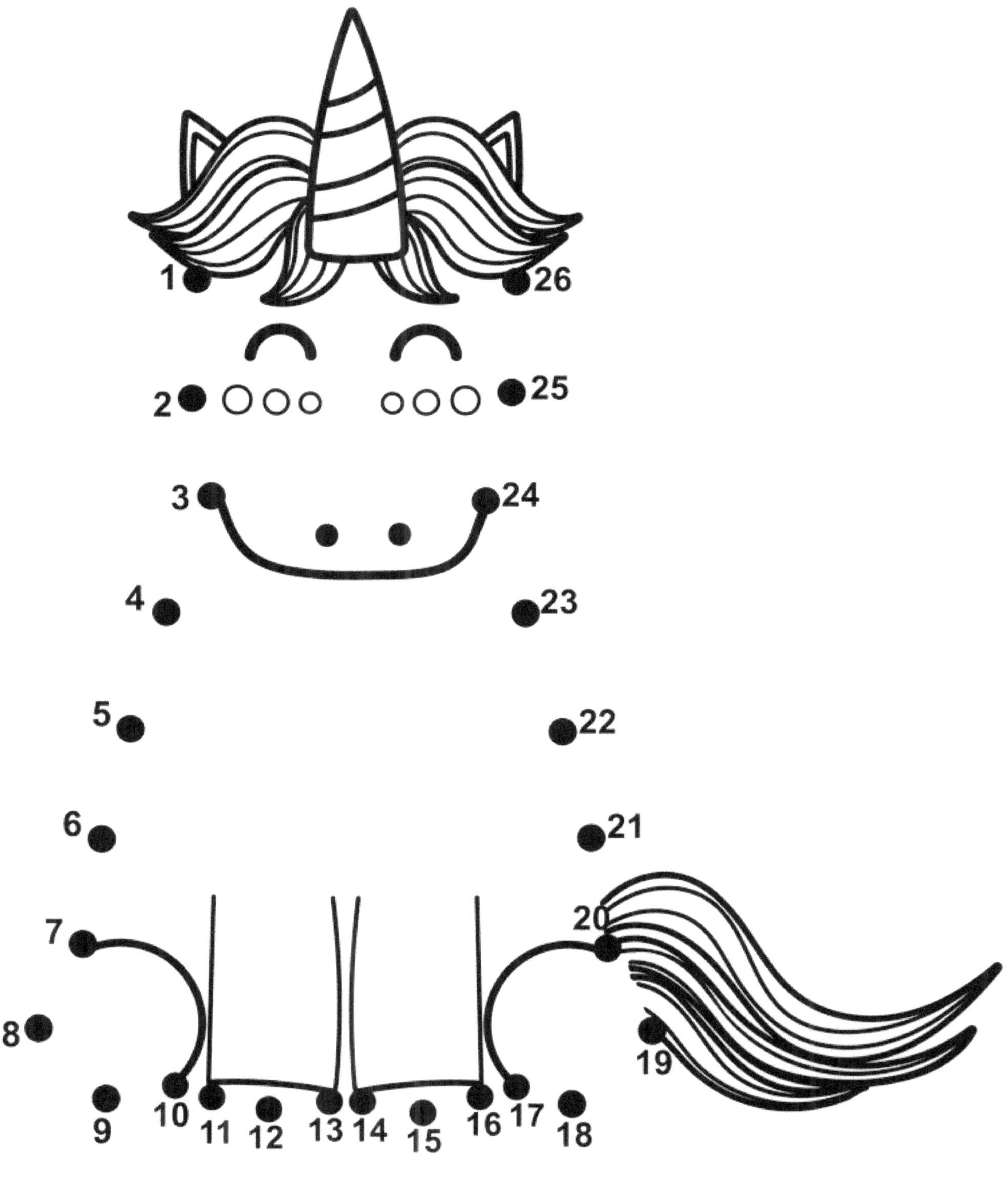

I am a legendary animal

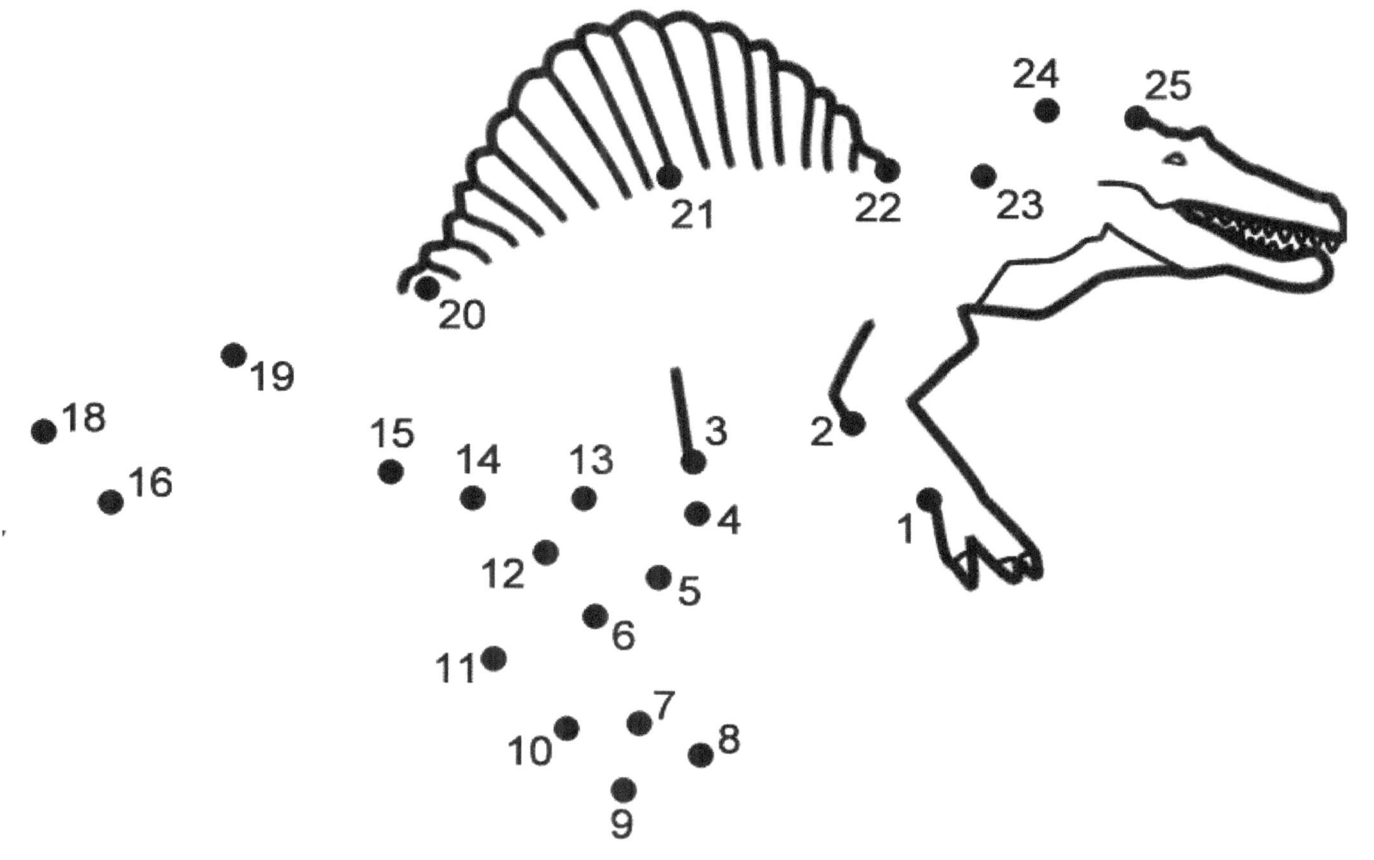

I had a life span of around
30 years

I ruled the Earth for more
than 160 million years

I give live birth and nurse my
young with milk

I went extinct about 66
million years ago

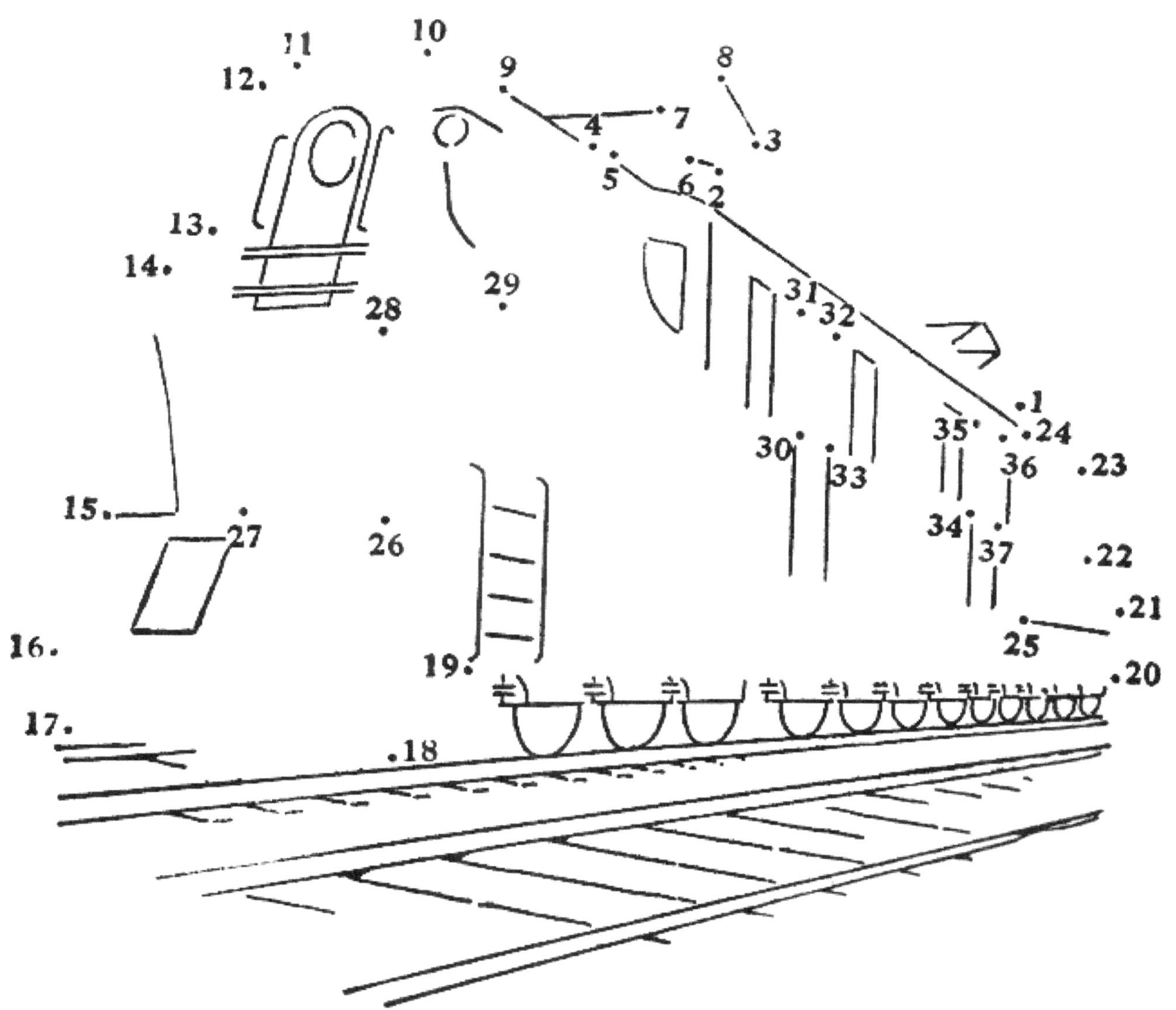

I was developed in Great Britain

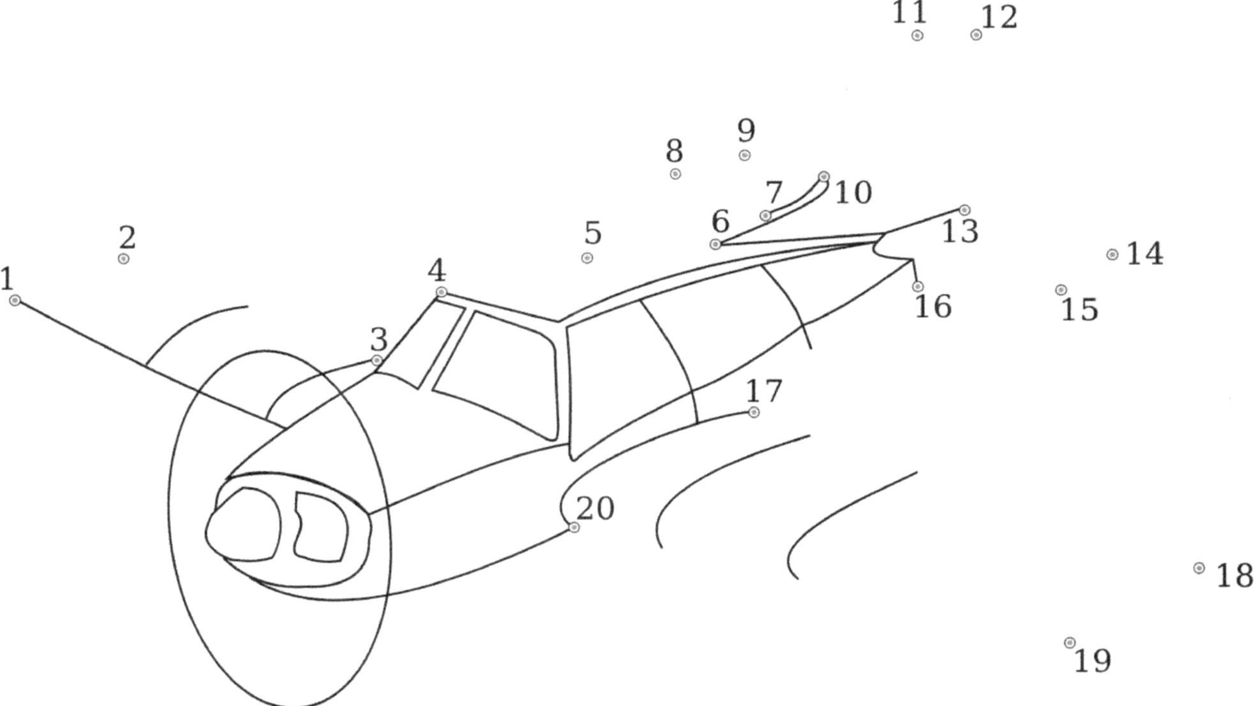

I was invented in 1903

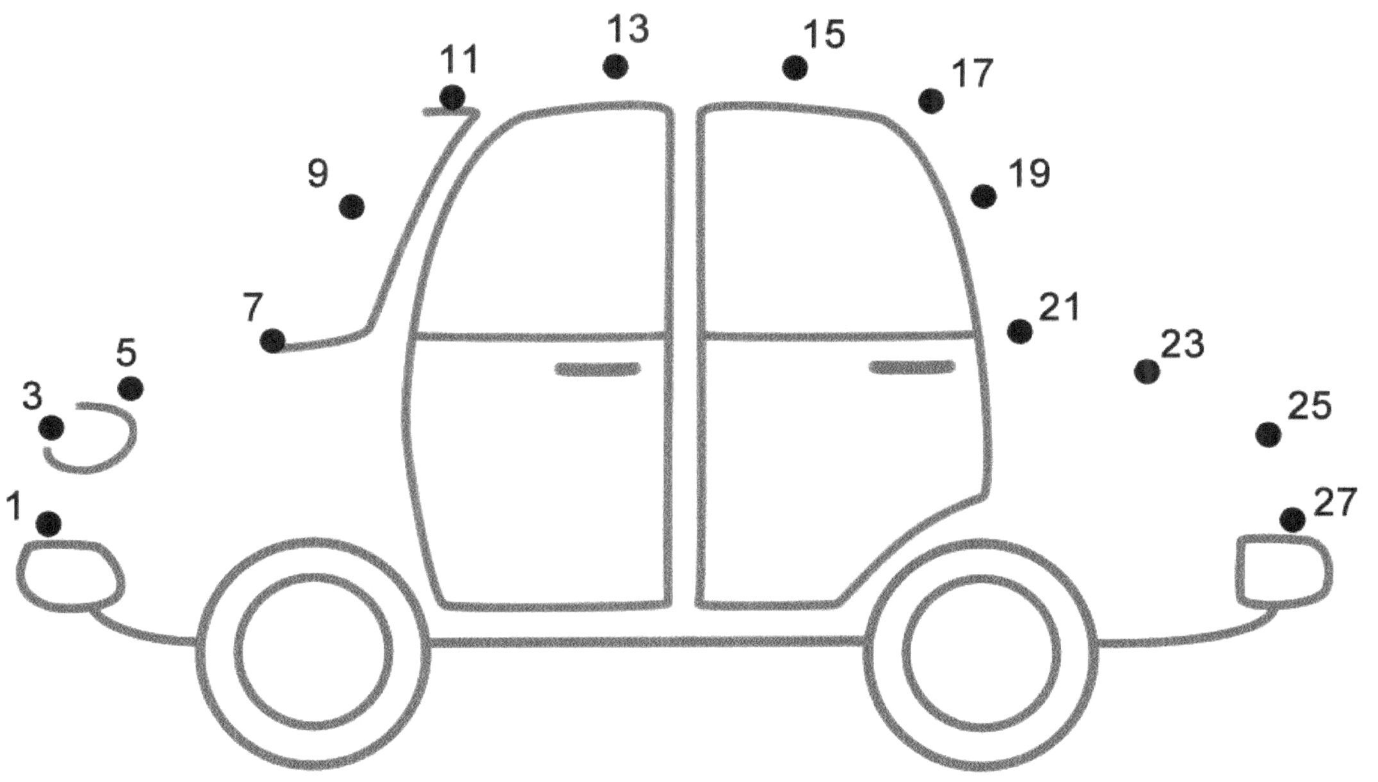

I was invented in 1885